Triumph over the Trials

Triumph over the Trials

COMPILED BY
Bridgett McGowen

BMcTALKS Press
4980 South Alma School Road
Suite 2-493
Chandler, Arizona 85248

Copyright © 2020 by Bridgett McGowen. All rights reserved.

No part of this publication may be reproduced, stored in a retrieval system, or transmitted in any form or by any means, electronic, mechanical, photocopying, recording, scanning, or otherwise without the prior written permission of the Publisher. Requests to the Publisher for permissions should be submitted to the Permissions Department, BMcTALKS Press, 4980 S. Alma School Road, Ste 2-493, Chandler, AZ 85248 or at www.bmctalkspress.com/permissions

The views expressed in this publication are those of each of the contributors; are the responsibility of each contributor; and do not necessarily reflect or represent the views of BMcTALKS Press, its owner, or its independent contractors.

Volume pricing is available to bulk orders placed by corporations, associations, and others. For details, please contact BMcTALKS Press at info@bmtpress.com

FIRST EDITION

Library of Congress Control Number: 2020909536

Paperback ISBN: 978-0-9998901-8-9

eBook ISBN: 978-1-7351192-2-9

Printed in the United States of America.

Dedication

For Aaron and Parker

Get Published!

"You should write a book."

Either you have heard that from someone else or you have said it yourself, but at BMcTALKS Press, we believe you should do it.

We take your dream from a great idea to a beautifully formatted book.

BMcTALKS Press is an independent publishing company that is fully committed to getting your non-fiction work published in a timely manner and providing you with a finished product that's professionally done and one of which you will be proud.

When you join the BMcTALKS Press family, you receive personal attention and one of the higher author royalties in the industry.

This will be one of the most exciting experiences ever.

You are an expert. Now it's time you let everyone know it.

Visit **www.bmctalkspress.com** today to get your FREE author's guide.

Let's print your passion!

Table of Contents

LETTER TO THE READER xi
FOREWORD xiii

Shonna Dent
Be Positively Persistent 19

Tabitha Evans
A Tough Decision May Be the Right Decision 35

Diane Gunderson
Be Present, Be Thankful, Be Grateful 51

Dr. Ana Lara
Stand Out ... Be Different 63

Chantell Wilson Link, PhD
Realize the Power of the Mindset 75

Bridgett McGowen
Hold Your Head High 85

Letter to the Reader

By late March of 2020, we all came to realize we were living in different times—times that pushed us out of our comfort zones.

When you thought about the global pandemic and what the future holds for you, there may have been uncertainty. Fear. Worry. Or you may have felt excited, optimistic, or even hopeful.

I get it.

I, too, experienced a mix of those emotions—sometimes I experienced all of them in the span of one day.

My husband, Aaron, is an essential employee. He is a manager with the light rail system in downtown Phoenix and had to report to work to ensure other essential workers had access to public transportation to get to *their* jobs. Of course, we worried about him going out every evening to work the second shift but were thankful on some level that, as a manager, he was able to monitor the rail system mostly away from others and in a safe location. Then we also have a kindergartener who had a first-time experience with homeschooling and who also missed friends, extra-curricular activities, and the life we used to live. Our family is not unique; much like countless others, for us, some days were definitely tougher than others and had me questioning how in the world to press through.

This book is a joint effort from select incredible members of my community who came together in April 2020 on Zoom—the meeting place of choice during the pandemic, right?!—to write chapters about our personal trials in an effort to encourage you to push through even when things are uncomfortable—even when pushing through is the last thing you want to do.

We answer the question "What is one of the biggest trials or challenges you have ever had, and how did you overcome it?" And we each give a piece of advice that lets you know the triumphs are always greater than the trials. Always.

Your challenges, roadblocks, and trials have nothing on you and your triumphs. Rise above, stay strong, be you. You can do anything. You can. Believe that.

-*B*

Foreword

What does the word "triumph" mean to you?

Is it simply a verb found in the dictionary? Is it a word rarely used in your daily vocabulary? Is it an experience we never even take the time to contemplate, or is it something more? When you speak or hear the word, does it evoke a feeling within that induces pride and a sense of accomplishment? Whether you believe it's none of those things or all of those things, one thing is for certain; when we do experience a sense of triumph, it is a deep-rooted feeling that is accompanied by a surge of emotions. If you are of the belief that it means nothing to you, then maybe you are still working towards overcoming your trials and simply haven't experienced your triumph ... yet.

We all have faced trials in our lives that have come in the form of obstacles although they may have manifested dissimilarly and to greater or lesser degrees. Yes, indeed, some of these obstacles may, in fact, even be the same for some of us but contrasting in how we perceive them. Whatever the case, when we find a means to overcome these trials, we feel a sense of pride, a sense of relief, and a sense of triumph that can only be induced by such a victory.

I have been fortunate enough to become a number one best-selling author, a life progression coach, a keynote speaker, and an entrepreneur. However, these triumphs did not come without trial. On the contrary, coming from a life of trials, I understand that some trials in life are difficult, to say the least, and don't seem fair. I understand that sometimes we may feel forsaken and are propelled to ask "Why me?" I also understand the most profound aspect of these trials, that no matter what they are, they can be overcome.

This book is the vision of Bridgett McGowen, award-winning international speaker, Forbes contributor, author, and publisher. After learning my life story, Bridgett felt inspired to help others that are experiencing trials in their lives in order to show them that whatever the obstacle, it is not insurmountable. She will lead you on a journey of trials to triumph through the eyes and experiences of multiple authors. It will help you realize that it's not what you go through but how you pull through.

Having worked with Bridgett on multiple projects as colleagues and now as friends, I can attest to her innate ability to deliver a powerful message that is capable of inducing positive change to those who need it and seek it. Bridgett will share with you insight into one of her biggest trials and give you a front-row seat as to how she overcame it. This book is not merely words to paper; it is a compilation of triumphant authors, granting you an intimate view into their most vulnerable times in life so as to render assistance to those who believe that their trials are greater than their triumphs. By title and by purpose, this book is a testament to the fact that triumphs can indeed overcome trials in any given situation.

One would normally tell you all the things that his/her work will do, but I won't do that. I've chosen to tell you what it won't. This book will NOT be your means to an end. It will not be the cure-all, fix-all to your problem. It will not even give you direction towards a possible solution to whatever you are going through. No, it will not do any of those things unless you allow it to. Read with an open mind and an open heart, and this book may be the "chicken soup for the soul" that you've sought your whole life and didn't even realize you needed until you read the last word on the last page.

I do not profess that change is easy nor do I want you to think that the change you seek will be too difficult. What I want to express is that it will take work and determination, and there is no overnight fix to all of the circumstances with which you are faced. You see, in life there is no elevator towards success; you have to take the stairs, but with time, effort, and determination, you can reach the top. The authors within this book have done exactly that, and their chronicles can serve as a blueprint to aid you in building your success story.

Our greatest abilities are sometimes discovered during our greatest trials. You are stronger and more capable than you have ever given yourself credit to be if only you are willing and ready to give yourself the opportunity. Read these words and grow with every sentence and every word. Realize that your present circumstances do not have to be the measure for your future. Build upon the foundation that this book can create for you, and do one last thing: let it teach you, guide you, and inspire you towards YOUR triumph.

With love and warmest regards to all,

Clinton Harris
Clinton Harris Coaching
CEO & Founder
www.clintonharriscoaching.com

Triumph Over the Trials

Be Positively Persistent
SHONNA DENT

Shonna's Trial

As an instructor and a program supervisor working for a higher education institution, student success was always at the forefront of my mind. There have been various instances in which I found myself presented with trials. One trial or roadblock, in particular, revolved around working towards setting up our college students for success in a way that had never been done before.

The college had always had a basic two-hour orientation that was held prior to a start day. In an effort to better prepare the new college students, I felt passionately that we should consider changing the way we oriented our students to the campus in order to better set them up for success. The orientation was basic and uneventful. The new students would get to see the admissions teams again and some other members of the campus that would say who they were and what their roles were. I felt deep in my heart that if we could prepare our students in a manner that set them up for college and career success prior to them starting their first course, that the students would feel better capable of making that big transition, would feel more confidence in themselves, and would know the support and resources available to them. All of this would lead to improved student retention and increased student outcomes.

In 2011 and again in 2013, I began asking and pushing that some consideration be given to revising orientation. I was proposing that we organize orientation and we ensure that all departments present what they can offer to the new students in the area of student support and resources. The campus would just say, "Shonna, why are you always wanting us to do more work?" "Shonna, it is just orientation; the students get what they need." Unfortunately, the decision had been made that no changes were going to be made to orientation.

I wondered why nobody could see the benefit of taking this risk, making this change? Why wouldn't they listen to me?

In January 2015, I took over the role of corporate director of academics. Woo hoo!! "I can finally make a bigger impact on student success" was my first thought. "Now, I can launch into my first big project and change orientation" was my second thought. I was so excited. I had been working towards this goal and opportunity since I started teaching at the college in 2005. As I was beginning to get the hang of my new role, I was the only person overseeing the academics for four campuses, I had many areas of academics that I needed to update and revise, and I began to face additional challenges.

Since moving to the C-suite I started to experience backlash, and I was hearing the negative remarks and comments being said about my move from the campus to the corporate office. "How did Shonna get that job?" "What did she do that was so special to get that opportunity?" "She's a woman." "She's too young." "She must have just been handed that position." "She must be someone's pet, so that has to be how she was moved into a corporate position." Etcetera, etcetera, etcetera. I had always prided myself with the reputation I had built. Obviously, my predecessor had believed in me enough to promote me. I had the reputation of a hard worker, a lover of the students, a motivated leader, and a contributing team player when I worked at the campus. Now that I was in my new role, it was apparent to me that I was going to have to start over and build trust with the campuses and that I was going to have to work harder to prove that I was "still me," that I shouldn't be treated any differently and that I would never treat anyone working at the campus differently.

This process of building my reputation back up took almost a whole year.

All while this was occurring, I still was mindful that I needed to overcome my fear of failure, my fear of being incompetent and not able to make a big impact. I needed to prove myself in a manner that I had never had to do before.

But first, and before I could put my plan into motion, I had A LOT of work I needed to do to get my own foundation solid and to rebuild my image, confidence, and reputation. It was so frustrating to think that I was still not able to initiate changes ad make the impact I knew I could make because the walls just kept popping up in front of me no matter which road I took.

Throughout 2015, I had been mentioning to the corporate management team that I wanted to change orientation. I had started sharing my ideas, hoping to get the support I needed to launch my idea. I had no bites. I received only negative feedback: "It will cost too much money." "The students are fine with what they are getting introduced to." "It would be too much work for the campuses." "What will the impact be?" "Can you prove it?"

Shonna's Triumph + Advice

The question I had to ask myself was "To whom do I really have to sell my idea?"

It had been six years, and still nobody was wanting to move towards a change. The corporate management team wasn't listening, and the campuses didn't see a need for a change. What was I going to do? After deliberating, brainstorming, and researching, I decided I needed to pull out the big guns and cross the line that a person working in and overseeing academics normally doesn't cross and that was to go straight to the people who coordinated orientation: Admissions.

Now, I write that with the utmost respect for admissions. It isn't to suggest that academics and admissions don't normally work together because they do. In academics, we just know that there is a line you do not cross—a line that differentiates between enrolling students versus teaching and retaining students. I knew that this was going to be extremely difficult, and I had to think about what I had already been through. I thought about the negativity, and I thought about the lack of support and buy-in. I made the decision to push forward with everything I had because I felt so strongly about how this change would impact our students in such a positive manner that I could not ignore it. Being positively persistent was going to be my secret weapon in order to win.

I got back on my horse and started my journey yet again. My new path was taking me straight to the director of admissions. At the time, this individual was pretty new to our organization, and much to my surprise, he was immediately bought-in. YES!! The next step was to team-up and sell my idea to our board of directors. Working with our director of admissions and our academic coordinator, I was able to get all my ideas out of my head and into a plan—an amazing three-day, nine-hour course that new students would attend the week prior to starting in their programs. Before I could sell the new course that would replace orientation, I needed marketing material, and I needed a syllabus; a lesson plan; ancillary materials; and a huge bag of goodies, aka "a toolkit." Once the three of us worked everything out and put everything together, including a new student welcome folder made with construction paper and decorated with markers, we were ready to go.

I was given the permission to present the new course to the entire corporate team and board members. Aside from my first keynote speech at a graduation in 2015, this was the most nervous I had ever been at work. I came to the presentation absolutely ready to kill It! Dressed to the nines, music playing, and PowerPoint presentation on deck. Even the seat placements included the custom-made welcome folders, tactile stations, and textbooks. Just imagine the butterflies I had; the amount of positive energy I was oozing; and the walk I walked as I strutted in, ready to sell with all my might. Cue the grueling presentation: During my presentation, I was asked many questions for which I had answers, but they were not the answers they wanted to hear. "What is the ROI?" "How much is this going to cost?" "We can't have all the department heads in this class. They have other jobs to do." "What do you mean 'all new students have to attend'?" "What do you mean 'we will lose a week of enrollments in order to launch this'?" My fear began to settle in, and I thought to myself "Shonna, you are stronger than you think. You are smarter than you give yourself credit for."

I told myself that I needed to break down their walls so they could truly see me, so they could actually feel my passion. I told myself to jump over my own wall—the wall that I had built—that was obviously hiding my potential and my confidence. I told myself to believe in myself.

Those twenty seconds I took to pause and collect myself were so very powerful. I immediately knew that the close of the presentation was going to seal the deal. I felt on fire. I felt absolutely exhilarated. I had positivity pouring out of myself. I envisioned a rushing river and threw my doubts and fears into it. I took a deep breath, put the biggest smile on my face and turned to the board of directors. I explained to them that I had a plan and that they would need to believe in me. I told them that we could pilot the new course at one campus instead of all four. I told them that they would need to trust me, to believe in me, and to have confidence in me and that I would accept nothing less.

The energy in the room begin to shift from the force of positivity that was exuding from my pores and from the fact that I was standing strong, poised with confidence, and that I was not going to back down this time.

Everyone in the room begin conversing about the possibility of the pilot project. I began taking notes on the white board, listening to their encouraging comments and suggestions.

The last five minutes of that meeting were AMAZING! Everyone was now on board. A plan of action was in the works, and I was overwhelmed with gratitude—gratitude for how I handled the situation. Gratitude that I never gave up, that ...

I had the strength to dig deep to find solutions and overcome the many obstacles that had been presented before me.

Fast forward three years; all four campuses started the new course within a very short time after the pilot course launched. Overall retention and student satisfaction dramatically improved. All in all, the entire project was a success—an adventure that began as a trial and ended with triumph.

I truly believe that one has to be positively persistent in life. Never let the negativity of others affect the impact that you know in your heart you want to make. Always remember to break down those walls, crawl under the walls, search for a way to get around the barriers that may try to block you from getting where you need to go. Remember who you are and what is important to you. Write affirmations, hold yourself accountable, and never ever give up. Last, but certainly not least, be sure to love yourself. #PositivelyPersistent

Shonna's Bio

Shonna Dent is an experienced educational professional with over fifteen years in higher education working to improve the lives of adult learners. She is a strong advocate for a diverse, inclusive, and innovative work and learning environment. As an extremely motivated and encouraging individual, Shonna is committed to helping others meet their career goals through leading, educating, training, and mentoring.

Shonna is an accomplished professional development trainer and public speaker having presented at numerous events and for various organizations including faculty development workshop training sessions at the

Professional Development Conference hosted by the Accrediting Commission of Career Schools and Colleges (ACCSC). Examples of some of the topics Shonna has presented include Student Engagement Strategies, Creating a Positive Learning Environment, Improving Student Retention and Outcomes, College Success Preparation, Building Student Leaders, Creating a Foundation for Success, Get Up Stand Up and Learn, Playing the Victim vs Being the Creator, Motivate and Elevate, Effective Communication for Online Education, Effective Leadership and Group Dynamics, Faculty Development Planning, Bucking the Trend in Educational Delivery, MindMapping for Effective Lesson Planning, Cultural Diversity and Conflict Resolution, and Instructional Leadership and Development.

Shonna considers herself a lifelong learner and is always looking to expand her knowledge. Her commitment to continuous learning is made evident by the over fifteen thousand hours of continuing education that she has completed since 1999, including recently becoming a Certified Education Professional of Excellence in the areas of leadership, campus operations, teaching, and online teaching. As a keynote speaker for various college graduation ceremonies, Shonna always gives the following advice: "I want you to remember that you need to always be coachable and teachable. Be open to learning, no matter what someone is trying to teach you, and don't forget to take notes and remember names. Don't shy away from going on crazy adventures; you never know what new and exciting things you will learn or who you will meet along the way. If you find a big wall in the middle of the path you are taking towards your goals, don't give up and turn back. Find a way past the wall whether you jump over it, go around it, under it, or through it, don't let it stop you."

Shonna has a master's degree in organizational leadership management focused in educational development and delivery from Colorado State University–Global and is an ACCSC Certified Accreditation Professional.

Shonna's true passion revolves around educating others in creating a fun and rewarding learning environment while keeping a positive and up-beat attitude. She believes in mentoring and training educators to enhance the skills they currently have and developing new skills that will assist them in creating the most dynamic educational environments possible. This passion results in improved student satisfaction, student retention, and student outcomes as well as changing the lives of others. Her passion for helping others has led her to a new project that she has coming on the horizon. She is taking all of the knowledge and experience she has gained over the past fifteen years of working in higher education and is starting her own consulting company, Framework Development.

Shonna lives in Colorado with her family and loves camping, hiking, and pretty much anything that has to do with the outdoors. When introducing herself in a new environment, she tends to break the ice by announcing that her two sons have coined her as "the best worm finder" because she finds the biggest and juiciest worms to use when fishing the mountain creeks.

A Tough Decision May Be the Right Decision

TABITHA EVANS

Tabitha's Trial

One of the biggest challenges I have had to overcome in my life is the belief that I am not good enough.

There was a time in my life when I was angry with myself for decisions I had made. I did not trust my instincts, and I felt like I had failed. I doubted myself and was in a perpetual state of self-punishment. For me, it was a dark place. It took some time for me to grow up and realize what I was doing to myself. Self-sabotage is what I came to call it.

It all started with my childhood. My mom and dad met in high school, fell in love, and she got pregnant with my brother when she was a senior in high school. My father was young and made really poor decisions that lead to brushes with the law. My mom pleaded to a court to not put my father in jail, and she said she would bring him to Arizona where she was from. Little did she know, he was an abusive alcoholic, and he wasn't faithful to her. I will not go into all the details; instead, I will share a few memories I believe affected my life.

I remember getting spanked really badly for eating my dad's Oreos when I was less than two years old. I remember lying on my stomach in pain, crying on a mattress on the floor and my brother consoling me, telling me, "Don't let them see you cry." This is something that has stuck with me my whole life. I somehow clung to that and found strength in not crying and being the tough kid who could take on anything.

It was when, one late night, my father brought home a woman, woke up my mom, and made her cook for him and his girlfriend when my mom decided to leave him. He tried to beat her again, and he had no idea what she had waiting for him. She had been taking karate lessons on her lunch break at work, and she gave him a whooping I am sure he hasn't forgotten, packed up us kids, and left him. It was a tough decision but the right one. She had also been abused by her father for being born hard of hearing and didn't want a childhood of abuse for us. She struggled on her own, raising two small children with little help from family who mostly living in Oregon. At times, she worked three jobs to provide for us and to ensure we never went without.

When I was in high school, my mom somehow found my dad, and we were all reconnected. My brother and I went to his house for a surprise visit. When we knocked on his door and he opened it, his first words were "How did you find me?" Based on that greeting, I am sure you can imagine how great that visit was. We saw each other the one time and spoke over the phone a couple times.

One day after school, I received a call from my dad's girlfriend at the time, yelling at me and calling me horrible names. I was in shock. I had no idea from whence this was coming. Wasn't she an adult? Who talks like this to a child? They had seen me walking home from school with my friends—friends they, apparently, would not have chosen for me. Up until that moment, I had no idea my dad and his girlfriend were racist. I had no idea who this monster was on the phone. My dad picked up where his girlfriend left off and said I wasn't his daughter, that my mom was a slut, and he had no idea whose kid I was. I was sick inside. Absolutely sick. How could this animal be my dad? I was raised around all ethnicities and grew up in a major metropolitan city where diversity was normal. I did not get it.

I was in tears, and I called my mom at work. She stayed very calm and said, "Oh yes you are definitely his daughter, and he will be sorry for this one." She walked over to the courthouse, that day and filed for child support. She didn't want any of his money before and didn't chase him down to get it. Now, it was different, and she was on a mission to prove a point and to get even. She took him to court and charged him for backpay, resulting in him having to pay child support for several years into my early adulthood.

During my late teens, I found myself repeating patterns of self-doubt. I felt like I was invincible and remorseless. I was looking for love and acceptance from anywhere I could get it and made horrible choices in boyfriends and friends in general. My mom was always supportive, but she was also busy. I lived a life of which I was not proud. I had no boundaries and didn't even know what boundaries were, which led to me allowing myself to be used and taken advantage of.

As a young adult I was sexually assaulted and was a victim of the date rape drug. While I was the one who was the victim, I somehow blamed myself, thinking "Maybe I was too nice to him" or "Maybe my clothes were too provocative." I couldn't believe this had happened to me, and I was so confused. At this time, I was in the military with a top-secret clearance and was not allowed to show any mental effects of being raped nor was I allowed to receive any counseling because receiving counseling would result in me losing my clearance as well as my job. It was a terrible situation, and it nearly crushed me. I was far away from my family and had little support. Again, I was being told "never let them see you cry." I turned to religion for support and got baptized.

I wanted to change. I wanted a new life. My heart was broken and needed mending.

Even after all this, I repeated self-sabotaging patterns, and it caused me to make poor decisions. I was wild and totally out of control. I found myself aggressive with pent-up emotions that would come out when I did not expect them. I was trying to tame it, but something was not right. I continued to do things of which I was not proud and somehow found myself afraid of what I had become. I started drinking too much and surrounding myself with people who were not going anywhere in life. I listened to the programming I had buried deep in my head, "The Committees," as I called it. The Committees would wake me up in the morning, and I could not turn them off. I would go over things in my head again and again. It was a vicious cycle.

I knew deep down that I was not where I was supposed to be. I did not fully realize my value or self-worth. I had allowed others to take advantage of my kind heartedness. I was all over the place yet nowhere.

I was afraid of making bad decisions, of failure. I was afraid the decisions of my past would haunt me forever and that there was no way I could get out from under this gray cloud over my head.

Then, one day, I met a guy at a restaurant where I was working. He asked me "What do you want to do with yourself in the future?" I told him my plans. "I want to return to college one day and get my degree in interior design." We had an amazing conversation, but I was in a relationship at that time; as such, we did not exchange contact information.

A year later, he came back to the restaurant, and we were having another amazing conversation. He asked me "Have you started school for interior design yet?" I replied, "No." Then he asked me, "Why?" I honestly could not give him an answer. I did not know why. Why *was* I still here? A year later! Had it really been a year? Was I wasting my life? Then it hit me.

I was afraid I wasn't good enough.

At that very moment I suddenly realized, I was the only one standing in my way. It hit me like a ton of bricks! Why was I holding myself back? I was frustrated, and I needed to free myself of the guilt onto which I was holding. I was ready to move forward. I felt stagnant and stale. It was definitely time to move on. I was good enough!

Fortunately, I have always had the loving support of my family. My mom has always been my rock and has supported me with anything I wanted to do. She always taught me through stories of her life, and one thing my mom always said is "If they can do it, you can do it." So, I did it. I called and got it all set up to start college. It was so easy! I was so excited to be embarking on a new adventure and pulling myself out of this rut.

In this moment of self-realization, I realized who my true friends really were. Once I moved myself out of stagnation, I realized the people I had surrounded myself with did not like my changes very much because it made them face the reality of their own situations.

My friends were not happy for me at all. They did not answer my calls anymore and did not understand why I did not want to go out anymore. The ones I did hang out with were different now. I was going places, and I know my self-discovery made them feel uncomfortable. We no longer connected, and I was ready to move on.

Some of the challenges I faced going back to school were learning how to be a student after so many years, changing my lifestyle to meet the needs of school, and finding my authenticity. Changing career paths from soldier to bartender to interior designer was a bit of a challenge, but I welcomed it. I decided who and what I wanted to be—authentically me. I rediscovered myself and the joy of life came in like a flood. I loved the new me! I had a new lease on life and was enjoying my journey again. I took pride in all I worked for. I took school seriously and got involved in everything I could. I was building my new life!

Fast-forward thirteen years. I am now married to that guy from the restaurant, and his name is Matt. I went to college, graduated with honors, had three amazing children, and I became the president of the professional society at my school. I shared my life and light through volunteerism and mentoring. I was selected to be on the state chapter board and eventually became the president. I have had my works published locally, regionally, and nationally, and I have worked on projects in my field all over the United States.

To this day, I continue to grow. Now, I am stronger than ever, and I love a good challenge! There will always be new mountains to climb however, if it scares me then I am definitely going for it.

I left my doubt and fear that I was not good enough in that restaurant thirteen years ago.

I look back now only to celebrate my challenges and to continue forward movement. I understand there are bumps in the road, but looking at them in a positive light changes everything.

Tabitha's Triumph + Advice

Believe in *yourself,* and do not give up!

From my own personal experience, triumphs are always greater than the trials. I have gone through many trials in my life. When I go through a trial, it feels like it will N E V E R end. It feels like the weight of the world is on my shoulders. I cannot imagine how I will make it through sometimes. Then I do, and when I do it feels A M A Z I N G!!

Let me give you an example: When I was in basic training to become a soldier in the United States Army, there were times when I did not feel like I could physically do any more. One day, in our first week, there we were getting "smoked" by our drill sergeants in a tiny room with our entire platoon nearly on top of one another. We could barely do pushups without touching each other. In their words, the drill sergeants wanted to make the walls sweat. We were doing physical exercise for what seemed like an entire afternoon, and we were going on little sleep; so we were already exhausted to begin with. We were doing burpees, pushups, mountain climbers—you name it. They wanted to break us. I know I was not doing proper pushups; there was no way I could. I was barely able to hold my body up off of the ground, and my arms were shaking uncontrollably. I was embarrassed about the physical shape I was in. I wanted my arms to stop shaking before others saw them. I felt so weak! However, I remember looking over to my left, and there was this really big muscular guy; and he was crying. I could not t believe it! I was worried about my arms collapsing and looking weak, and he was crying.

In that moment, I felt so empowered. Here I was this scrawny little girl, but I was hanging mentally! I found strength in that moment, and I didn't stop. I held my body up while trembling and kept going. I will never forget the feeling I had that day. These are the moments that define us and build our beliefs in ourselves.

Use these trials for personal growth. When you look back at the trials you have gone through, you see them in a different light. You see them from a new perspective. When the battle is behind you, you can take the time to learn from it. During this time, you will gain so much insight. Take the time to dissect it, go through the process, and figure out what you realized from the overall experience. Even in the worst of experiences, you will gain something. Not all circumstances are the same. You may even laugh about some of them.

What I learned from this experience was that we all have different strengths and knowing who you are and understanding your strengths will help you believe in yourself. When you are tested with trials, you will learn that of which you are capable.

In fact, you will overcome situations you never thought were possible.

Becoming stronger and more self-aware are just two things you will gain. It is pretty incredible if you think about it! Look at the process from the perspective of what am I going to learn or gain from this instead of feeling beat down about it.

When you learn to believe in yourself you will start to understand that you have a lot more control than you thought you did. You can move mountains! All you have to do is decide you are going to do it and then DO IT! After all, you may think you have nothing left to give, and someone else seems to be doing better than you when in all reality, it may be that they are actually beaten down and crying.

"Whenever you find yourself doubting how far you can go, just remember how far you have come. Remember everything you have faced, all of the battles you have won, and all of the fears you have overcome." - Author Unknown

Tabitha's Bio

Award winning, interior designer, Tabitha Evans is an established and well-respected member of the interior design industry. She is the principal interior designer of Tabitha Evans Design, a design studio based in Arizona. Tabitha is married and has three children, a dog, and a tortoise. When she is not designing, she loves traveling, cooking, gardening, and fashion.

Tabitha Evans believes interior design is fundamental; it transforms lives. She believes interior design can impact your health, and she wants you to feel great in your space. She believes in humanizing the living, working, healing environments and is passionate about what she does!!

As a member and past president (2017-2018) of the Arizona North Chapter of the American Society of Interior Design (ASID), she loves volunteering and giving back to the community. She is currently holding the title of Government Affairs Representative to the board for the Arizona North Chapter of ASID. She has received several prestigious awards and has been published in magazines locally, regionally, and nationally.

She attended school at the Art Institute of Phoenix where she graduated with honors with a Bachelor of Arts degree in interior design. Tabitha is an innovator, creator, and visionary. She believes, through collaboration and communication from everyone who will use the space, the outcome of the design will be something truly special.

Tabitha is also a veteran of the United States Army. She spent over six years as a signals intelligence analyst. Tabitha Evans's designs are influenced by her extensive world travels. She has lived in Asia, Europe, and the United States. Her current mission, outside of interior design, is mentoring others so they can learn from their trials and to help them to see all of the great opportunities before them.

Be Present, Be Thankful, Be Grateful

DIANE GUNDERSON

Diane's Trial

One of the biggest challenges I've faced in my lifetime was going through a divorce after spending twenty-three years with my best friend, my husband. They say what doesn't kill you makes you stronger, and I have to say I am now a firm believer in that saying. At the time, when the world was crashing down around me, I didn't think I could see the light of day ever again. I spent countless hours and days crying and going through each stage of grief. I like to think of myself as an optimist and someone who typically looks at the glass as half full, but during those dark days, weeks, and months, the glass was as empty as it could be. At the time this was going on in my personal life, there were also challenges nationwide with the industry in which I work, for-profit education, and as a result, our organization had to make some tough decisions and had to close two of our college campuses due to lower enrollment.

Getting up each and every day and putting one foot in front of the other proved to be a challenge. On a daily basis, I told myself I had to do this not only for myself but for my future. I spent a lot of time crying in the bathroom at work but lifted my head up after my pity party, touched-up my makeup, and walked out the door believing I could survive.

The triumph occurred when I realized I had to keep living life in spite of the grief, despair, and sadness I was experiencing. I had to think about my family, and this was much bigger than me. I turned to my faith and those in my circle who could support and help me. As a result, I triumphed over the despair and devastation. Today, I continue to work on myself and try to become a better version of myself in spite of falling short many days.

I strongly believe that life will challenge us only to see if, in the face of adversity, we can find ways to overcome that adversity. I want to encourage people to find the good in spite of a bad situation and remind us all that things can—and oftentimes do—get better if we just focus on the positive.

One of my favorite quotes that I shared with a colleague back in the 80's when we first worked together at another college is "Don't worry about tomorrow. God is already there," which comes from the book of Matthew.

Keeping the faith is something that has sustained me during good times and bad times, and as a result, I will continue to do so daily. Look for the triumph in the midst of the trial....it may be buried, but it will surface eventually. Wait for it, or better yet, go out and seek it!

D-I-V-O-R-C-E, as the song says, it happened this way: It was unexpected and certainly one of the most blindsiding events of my life. When others in my life learned of the divorce, they too were shocked, indicating this is something no one would have expected. I didn't see it coming. Perhaps I should have, but I didn't.

My biggest question is WHY? Why did this happen? Why did he want to leave me? I know he said he was unhappy, but I was happy. What happened? When did he decide this is what needed to happen? I thought we were best friends who loved each other. How long ago did he decide this?

Can I fix it? Can I repair what is broken? Am I the one who is broken? Am I a failure?

Will we get back together soon or even someday in the future? Can we still be friends after this?

There were so many fears. I was afraid of being alone. I was afraid that no one would ever want to be with me or love me again. I was afraid of being a failure. (Did I mention this was my second marriage, and now I really felt like a failure?) I was afraid of my financial future and whether I would be able to survive on my own. Where would I live? I felt useless and like I was not good enough for anyone.

What was most frustrating was being blindsided by this event—the fact that I could not make this marriage work. The fact that it happened. The fact that I could not get him back into my life.

Being angry frustrated me. Crying all the time and feeling sorry for myself frustrated me. Going through the motions and feeling out of control of my life frustrated me.

However, I have an amazing family that supported me all the way through the process. I also have an amazing counselor who has been my sounding board for the past three years. I have an amazing group of people whom I met through a divorce group at my church and who still remain by my side two and a half years later. We all experienced the same event in our lives, and although our stories are all different, there was a common thread that held us together and that continues to hold us together today. These will be lifelong friends in my circle.

I also had great support from my organizational team at work—owners, CEO, regional directors, and staff—once I felt safe to share what had happened.

My light comes from my faith and the love of my family. Joy has been longer in coming, but after almost three years, I find joy in living again—somedays more than others—and I look forward to the future and what lies ahead for me. I no longer fear being alone. I have my faith, my family, and my friends. My strength has been tested again and again throughout this time, but just when I think I am weak and worried about life and what lies ahead, something good happens. As they say "Everyday may not be good, but there is something good in everyday;" and now I make that my mission to find that something good every day. I have a plaque with this saying in my home to remind me to be present, be thankful and be grateful. Tomorrow is a new day!

Diane's Triumph + Advice

In order to provide advice on how to triumph over the trials in life, I will reflect on how I have been my entire life and provide the reader with a glimpse into my belief system. I have always thought of myself as an eternal optimist or a glass half-full kind of gal. I have had my share of challenges but never felt as though there was something through which I could not persevere and overcome, and sharing my trial to triumph story is no different.

Giving up on myself while I was struggling through this divorce was certainly a thought that crossed my mind on many of the cloudy, dark days through which I trudged, but perseverance got me through those days. I had to remember who I was, and in spite of negative thoughts and fears that often times occupied my mind, I had to remember that I needed to be present for my family. I am a person who loves to live by quotes, and as my Momma always says,

> *"If the good outweighs the bad, stick it out and make it work."*

I believe I lived that affirmation many times since the divorce as well as while I was married for so many years. In addition, I continue to persevere in an industry that, for many years, has been under the microscope and has had to overcome so much adversity.

One thing that helped me get through my trial and appreciate the triumph was surrounding myself with people who truly cared about me, loved me for who I was, and accepted me without judgement. I devoted time each day to reading self-help books, leadership books, daily devotionals, and the Bible and researching opportunities to better myself and my situation. I attending classes supporting divorce care through my church (many institutions offer this class). I did the homework and shared my story with others during and after the classes. I forced myself to be social and spend time with others even when I was not feeling like doing so. I did not hesitate to reach out and ask for help when I needed it.

Stay positive. Believe in yourself. "Keep the faith" as my daughter always says, and learn to pick up the pieces and start over no matter when the trial occurs in your life.

We do not know what life will hand us, but as long as we stay positive and persevere, we can accomplish anything and overcome any trial which will lead to a TRIUMPH!

Don't give up...You've GOT THIS!

Diane's Bio

Diana Gunderson currently serves as the vice president of education at IBMC College in Fort Collins, Colorado. She has been at the college for almost seventeen years and has spent over thirty years in higher education. She loves working with students and faculty and has been a part of the executive team for more than ten years, working with the CEO and owners. Prior to working at IBMC College, she worked as the director of continuing education for National Technological University (NTU). She worked for NTU for thirteen years in distance educational training focusing on areas of leadership and professional development. After leaving NTU, Diana co-owned Training Systems Network and produced and directed short televised leadership training seminars with her co-owner and hosted a talk show featuring CEOs and leaders from various organizations sharing their success stories.

Diana graduated cum laude in 1999 from Regis University with a Bachelor of Science degree in business administration with a minor in communications. She has completed several master's level courses in management at Regis University. Diana is a graduate of the 2012 Leadership Academy of IBMC College. She currently serves as the executive secretary for the Colorado ACT Council.

Diana enjoys writing curriculum, assisting instructors in preparing for classes, presenting at faculty in-service meetings, and supporting students inside and outside of the classroom. She enjoys teaching classes at IBMC in the business administration and accounting degree and allied health degree programs.

Diana grew up in Indiana, moved to Colorado over thirty-five years ago, and calls Colorado home. She enjoys spending time with her two adult children, family members, and friends. She enjoys being outdoors when the weather is nice, enjoys reading magazines and self-help books, and loves shopping and hanging out with family and friends. Her favorite motto is live, love, laugh!

Stand Out ... Be Different

ANA LARA, N.M.D.
NATUROPATHIC MEDICAL DOCTOR

Ana's Trial

Life works in very mysterious ways. I am currently experiencing the biggest challenge. I'm in my second year of business, but after year one in business, I went through a business partnership dissolution—not fun, by the way. However, I am grateful for my decision. The week I officially received notice of the legal changes going through with the business is the week of the initial coronavirus shutdowns, and there was massive hysteria. Toilet paper, Clorox, and hand sanitizer shortages happened within a couple of days! I was just seeing the light at the end of the tunnel; I was excited to shift my business in the direction it was intended to go. I'm a healthcare provider, and I initially I saw the opportunity for my business to take off. This was the best time for people to take their health more seriously, and I had a ton of ideas. So, what's the big problem?

A week after the quarantine was set, I began to get calls and messages from colleagues asking me, "Are you going to close your clinic? I am and a lot of other doctors are too. We cannot risk being a vector for this virus. It would cause legal issues." I thought to myself, "Why would I close my business/clinic if I am an essential worker? I can help people to stay healthy and optimize their health as much as possible with natural and safe means." I had my guard down. I did not take notice that their fear was becoming contagious, and soon it would take over me.

Within days, I went into a mental panic—the type that no one could see from the outside. This is even worse because from the outside, you look like you are calm and in control only to find yourself having an internal storm ...

like Elsa from the movie *Frozen*. I feared if I had to temporarily close my clinic, then this would lead me to eventually having to close my entire business. I soon found myself feeling like a victim and telling myself "This is it. I have worked so hard to get to this point to lose everything!" I went from feeling overwhelmed to becoming angry at the world. How could this be happening right this moment just as I was about to spread my wings to fly?

I allowed myself to get all this out of my system. By day three, I pulled myself up and forced myself out of my house and back into my clinic. The world was diligently working to convert their businesses to operate online. I was already set-up to offer telemedicine, but my problem was I did a lot of hands-on therapies that required a live person in front of me. I still forced myself to look at operating online and shifted to a much better mindset. I reminded myself "Ana, go with the flow. Go at the rate you can work. Be gentle, be optimistic, and just keep swimming." (Okay, I have kids, so I have a lot of kid movie analogies; but they really inspire me.) I did some online webinars and attracted some clients, but I was not feeling fulfilled. This was the time I decided to stop everything for a while.

I took about a week, and I slept a lot! Sleep resets my brain; it's super helpful. I spent time with my children and played. I meditated two to three times a day. I listened and read things that inspired me. I turned to mentors whom I highly respect and admire, and one of them made a huge impact as he always does. His name is Jesse; he is a healer to whom I go, and he told me "Why are you so stressed and worried? God didn't bring you this far to let you fail. You were put there to help people heal, so go and heal. He didn't say it would be easy. All this to die for. But at the end, God will ask you 'What good did you do with the time I gave you? What did you teach others? What did you learn from others?'" He was straight and direct to the heart. I shook off the victim mentality, the fear, and the uncertainty, and I got back to work.

I continued to see clients in my clinic, taking precautions of course. But then again, I always took all necessary sanitary precautions; I am a smart and cautious person. My business was still significantly impacted by the quarantines and had far fewer clients coming in. However, the clients who were reaching out for help and who wanted to come in were in need of mental and emotional support. As I continued to be of service to my clients and anyone with whom I came into contact, I become a beacon of light. They were turning to me for guidance and for reassurance that everything would be okay. I continued to be a source of empowerment and inspiration to them during these troubling times. The more people I helped, the more I learned and the more empowered I became. Seeing my clients have peace and become more grounded in themselves is what lifted me up. I held the mentality of "Like attracts like" and "Light attracts light." I realized this was only the beginning of a much larger movement of a collective consciousness. My business began to shift the moment my thinking and attitude shifted, and my business continues to grow.

My meditations helped me to get clear.

I needed to keep myself clear of fear and any outside noise. I realized I have everything I need within myself. I just need to continue to take action and put things into motion.

Ana's Triumph + Advice

Building a business is like giving birth to a baby. The pain of the contractions builds stronger and stronger with time. There is this part of you that wants it to end, and you feel like you cannot do it anymore. You want to quit. But you are too far into the process, so you change positions and do breathing techniques to get you through the pain. Some will take an epidural to get through it. The time finally comes, and the mom is ready to push that baby out. It's exhilarating; the mom is tired and is waiting to see that little face and hold her baby. Finally! The mom is filled with love, joy, and peace to see a healthy baby only to go home and not sleep because there is a crying baby, or she is up with feedings and changing diapers. The parents still love the baby regardless. The cycle continues, and whether you are a female or male, the experience is shared.

Business is no different than the process of having a baby. There are difficult moments that cause stress and some level of mental/emotional pain, but if you push through those difficult moments and focus on the solution, you will enjoy the end results. Depending on the type of business you have, the end result may differ, but the process is the same. Find ways to readjust yourself and your business to get to the next level or when you face a challenge.

Don't quit; seek help.

As I write this, we are experiencing a pandemic of SARS-CoV-2 (also known as coronavirus disease 19), many businesses were asked to shut-down. While I am in an industry that is considered essential, many other doctors were closing their offices and offering telemedicine. I had to be creative with my processes and also ask myself "What is my why for doing the work I do?" While I have answered this question many times in the past, this time the current events gave me a different perspective. I could coward down and be in fear, or I can come up with unique solutions to help people during this pandemic. Many would need health and wellness guidance and support, especially in mental health. I chose the latter. While the majority of medical offices were closed in the medical plaza where my office is located, I continued to go in every day to service people, be it in-person or virtually. I had to be a voice of reason, comfort, and guidance during these times. There were too many people panicking, depressed, or anxious. I was okay being different and unique to service my patients.

Be okay to stand out and be different; that is your unique gift.

Really understand your "Why?" During difficult moments, it is very easy to lose sight of why you do what you are doing in life. Print it up and put it in front of you where you can see it every day. This will constantly be a reminder and a way to reignite your fire and passion for what you do. It has to be a strong conviction—something that you are super excited to do, and it has to fulfill a need that no one else is doing. What will set you apart from your competitors? Be exceptionally you.

It is through the struggles and the trials of tribulation that you can give birth to great ideas that service the community in a much better way. In order to master life or a business, you need to master yourself.

Ana's Bio

Dr. Ana Lara is a Phoenix, Arizona native, a community she has served over her lifetime and is a licensed naturopathic physician in the state of Arizona. Dr. Lara graduated with honors from the University of Phoenix with a Bachelor of Science in Business/Finance and a Master of Business Administration. Due to her journey with her own health, she became interested in nutrition and holistic health. She reversed Type II Diabetes and Hashimoto's Thyroiditis, an autoimmune thyroid condition, on her own using diet, botanical medicine, and other natural therapies. After regaining her health, she attended Southwest College of Naturopathic Medicine and Health Sciences in Tempe, Arizona and earned her doctorate in naturopathic medicine.

Prior to becoming a naturopathic medical doctor, Dr. Lara worked in various businesses in law, finance, banking, financial planning, real estate, and academia. This helped her with founding her own company later on.

She is the founder and owner of Raíces Naturopathic Medical Center, PLLC in Phoenix. Dr. Lara takes an interest in treating the whole person, not just treating symptoms. She uses the most effective natural treatments in conjuncttion with the latest medical research. At Raíces, it's a priority to create a healing and calming atmosphere where there are no wait times, and the time is invested in listening to the patient and providing education or therapies. People are heard; validated; and helped in deep, profound ways.

Her practice's focus includes family medicine, pediatrics, women's health, clinical nutrition, metabolic disorders, pain management, mental/emotional conditions, endocrine disorders, neurological disorders, chronic, and autoimmune diseases including chronic pain. She is an expert in preventing and treating Type II Diabetes, thyroid disorders, and autoimmune conditions.

Dr. Lara knows first-hand what chronic disease can do to one's quality of life, which is why she is passionate about disease prevention and reversing disease. As a wife and mother, she knows how much women tend to over commit and focus the least on their own personal health. This is why Dr. Lara reaches out to women and empowers them to take control of their life and health so they can build healthier and happier families by engaging all members of the family. She does so by addressing the mind, body, and spirit through healthy lifestyle changes.
Dr. Lara is a member of Arizona Naturopathic Medical Association (AzNMA), American Association of Naturopa-

thic Physicians (AANP), and Pediatric Association of Naturopathic Physicians (PedANP). Dr. Lara is an advocate for her patients and an advocate who brings forth a new wave of medicine that has a focus on patient-centered care while using a natural and holistic approach.

Realize the Power of the Mindset

CHANTELL WILSON LINK, Ph.D.

Chantell's Trial

Overcoming Challenges of Blended Families: Can We All Get Along?

While reflecting on my life and reminiscing on some of the challenges and obstacles that are now in my rearview mirror, I proudly began to realize that I am a strong individual who never allows negative circumstances to hinder my progress even when, at times, I feel like giving up. During this reflection, I quickly realized that although there were many trials, my trials did not ultimately occur until adulthood as my childhood years were some of the best years of my life.

So, now fast forward to adulthood where, in my mind, I have it "going on," accomplishing many things in life—a doctoral degree, executive leadership positions, memberships to exclusive clubs, awards, recognitions and more—however, my greatest accomplishment in life was starting my own family, creating my own traditions, and establishing my legacy. The joys of being a wife, mother, daughter, and sister in-law brought forth meaning to life, however, although as rewarding as it might be, it most definitely comes with many challenges, especially when one has entered into a blended family as a result of divorce and second marriages, which is what I will spend some time on. While remarrying was exciting, one could not have anticipated the challenges of blending families or learning a "new way" of running a household, learning new family structures, and figuring out personalities or behaviors to which you just were not accustomed. Having a new male figure discipline your child or feeling as though you are only an "observer" with your new bonus children created some very awkward and sometimes upsetting moments.

Experiencing these situations created great angst and often made me question "What the hell am I doing?" But, fortunately, I was able to snap back and refocus that energy on positive thinking, and I explored various avenues and strategies that could help the family and keep everyone sane. Some key strategies that helped me with my new family were …

… Prioritizing my marriage and ensuring that all were on the same page and that we were somewhat agreeable or at least have an understanding.

Putting my marriage first and not allowing it to take the back seat to everything else going on in my life was key.

We often find ourselves in this position: kids first, work, and then our spouse in this exact order. Please trust and believe that this will create much resentment. If this is going on in your household, STOP now, have the conversation with your spouse, and reprioritize things.

Everyone in the household will benefit from this and will foster growth in the relationship as well as assist with you being on the same page.

... Recognizing and accepting everyone's background and upbringing and how it influences decisions.

The beautiful thing is we are all unique beings. No two people are made the same. We're not clones—at least not as of yet. We all think and act differently, and men and women are definitely not wired the same. We come from different backgrounds and, unfortunately, we were not built or trained by our parent(s) or guardian(s) to read minds. We cannot realistically expect our spouse to always understand our perspective and we must be willing to accept this.

... Ensuring that communication maintained a level of civility.

Face it—nothing will ever get accomplished if one or both parties are always disgruntled, angry, and pissed off. While arguments and disagreements are inevitable, one must be respectful and make sure that words are not damaging or are not meant to bring the other party down. Remember, this is the person you fell in love with. You "should" not and do not want to hurt or tear him/her down.

... Seeking guidance from counselors/ministers with whom both parties feel comfortable with sharing their thoughts and feelings in a non-judgmental setting.

Reaching out for guidance often shows growth in the relationship. We do not have all of the answers, and we should not pretend to have them. Soliciting guidance from a non-judgmental party and not your close relative is extremely important. Ultimately, you are seeking support through research-proven, successful resources to strengthen your relationship.

While almost all marriages have their challenges, I found that it was most important to accept the fact that there are challenges, identify them, and work to address them together as a team.

Chantell's Triumph + Advice

Just Say "No" to Doom and Gloom and "Yes" to a Positive Mind and Unwind

Many people have been programmed to think that you must be PERFECT, you can't fail, and that failure is a sign of weakness. On the other end of the spectrum, you have those who have thrown in the towel, who are sulking, and who believe they will never be successful or will never accomplish anything in life. Over the years, as I have grown and developed, I have realized the power of the mindset. If one believes he/she will do well and put forth the effort, then he/she more than likely will do well. If one believes he/she will not do well, then he/she more than likely will not.

As simple as it sounds, changing your mindset and having a positive attitude will contribute to achieving many things in life including a successful marriage. Taking bad experiences and using them for the good is a great place to start. For example, I choose not to look at my first marriage as a failure but as two individuals who simply grew apart and who were blessed and able to create a handsome, kind, and intelligent young man. In this situation, I choose to focus on the positive outcome as we both ultimately had many successes.

Also, instead of comparing parenting skills or complaining about what works and what does not work in our blended family, we have accepted that we have different points of view. And while we differ, let us simultaneously regroup and develop practices that work best for *our* new family and not remain married to how things were done in the past.

Being forward-thinking and maintaining a positive mindset eliminates unnecessary stress and often sets the tone for any situation in which you find yourself.

While we are human and things are not always going to go as planned, my advice is to acknowledge and recognize that there will be challenges, however, use them as learning tools, lessons learned, and strengthening opportunities.

Maintaining a positive mindset will help you successfully manage many things throughout life while positioning you to take control of your life.

Chantell's Bio

Dr. Chantell Wilson Link is an executive in higher education, currently serving as assistant provost for academics at Texas Southern University in Houston, Texas. Prior to this role, Dr. Link served as the associate vice chancellor of student success for one of the largest and fastest-growing community college systems in the nation, serving over 95,000 students.

Dr. Link's experience spans outside of Texas where she worked for the Louisiana Community and Technical College System as the associate vice president for enrollment management, providing leadership in student services for thirteen community and technical colleges located throughout the state of Louisiana that had a combined enrollment of more than 105,000 students.

She's held various leadership roles in higher education including vice president, executive director, and dean of academics, and she currently teaches graduate level courses in cultural diversity, ethics, and counseling.

Dr. Link is also passionate about community outreach and development where she has developed leadership programs designed to help mentor and groom young leaders. She has also developed leadership programs for a local chamber of commerce and has established an African American student success taskforce focused on success and completion for minority students.

Dr. Link has also been actively involved with several organizations including the Fort Bend County Chapter of Links, Incorporated; Alpha Kappa Alpha Sorority, Incorporated; and Jack and Jill of America. She has served on the Acres Home Chamber of Commerce Board, Aldine Scholarship Foundation Board, and Near Northwest Management District Board.

Dr. Link has presented in various settings on education and mental health issues such as bipolar disorder and has published research on leadership styles. Dr. Link is a native of Dallas, Texas and a graduate of Prairie View A&M University and Capella University with degrees in counseling and psychology. She is married to Ivan Link, and they have three children, Michael Hines, Sydney Link, and Bria Link.

Hold Your Head High

BRIDGETT McGOWEN

Bridgett's Trial

In 2008 or so, I had a conversation with a girlfriend who was in the process of fostering and adopting three children. You know how it is with girlfriends—we offer and ask for advice on *everything*. Therefore, it was no surprise when she asked for my advice as it related to her foster-to-adopt situation.

I recall telling her to make it a priority that she be as honest with her children as possible, telling them the truth from day one. Day. One. (Make sure you read those two words with serious emphasis!) It was a good conversation until our talks made their way around to the birth certificate.

But let us pause for a moment before going on.

Since we are on the topic, when was the last time you looked at your birth certificate? Go get it.

Look at it. Look at this official document long and hard. Is there anything amiss?

Does everything look in order? State, city, and county of birth. The name of the facility at which you were born. Date of birth. Time of birth. Parents' names. It all looks legit, right? But ...

What if ...

What if it is all a lie?

What if the name you were given at birth is actually different from what appears on your birth certificate?

And what if those details about you being born to that mother in that facility is also a not true? What if all these details are ostensibly based on a lie? Or if "lie" is too assertive, then what if these details are not 100% accurate?

As my conversation with the friend continued to make its way through the ins and outs of an adoptee's birth certificate, I shifted into keeping-it-real Bridgett mode because I had actually conducted research in this area. I told her how appalled I was that, based on what I had learned, in the instance of an adoption, a birth certificate can be generated with new details and filed to appear as an official and original accounting of the beginning of a person's life. This was the driving force behind my insistence that she be generous with telling the truth because that document can be anything but the truth for an adoptee. The homework I had completed on the adoption front produced for me plenty of questions surrounding it.

How can a document of vital statistics be revised so the child's name is not what it was on the day she/he was born? In the instance of an adoption, both the child's mother's and father's names are changed on the birth certificate where the biological parents' names are replaced with the adoptive parents' names, and everything else remains the same. How can this be done with no designation that this file—this birth certificate—has been generated in this altered format as a result of an adoption?

Surprisingly, the friend essentially laughed in my face as if I was some sort of a fool, offering a response that equated to "Of course, that would be done in the case of an adoption! What do you expect, that they're going to slap a 'You Are Adopted' sticker on it?!"

(Okay. Pause for another moment. That response—that response right there—is why, more times than not, I keep my opinions and questions to myself because the outcome is usually my ruminations are considered absurd when I believe there is merit to them. You do not have to agree, but at least give the thought an ounce of serious consideration rather than to dismiss or laugh at it.)

So, sure; the premise here is all of this is for the benefit of a child who cannot make rational, sound choices of this magnitude. Without question, the actions are not malicious, nor are they intended to cause harm; in fact, the child is the one on whose behalf everyone is acting to give her or him a chance.

But ...

What if you lived well into adulthood, and the person you thought you were all this time, the name you've been called all your life, the parents you thought were your biological parents all this time were not? What if none of it was true?

Your beginning and entrance into this world—the start of your history—is edited. It is partially erased, and you are told nothing about it.

That is what happened to me.

It was in 2006—years after entering adulthood, years after earning my high school diploma and my bachelors and master's degrees, and more than half a year after getting married—when I received confirmation that I was indeed adopted and that the names that appeared on my birth certificate were not the names of my biological parents but were the names of adoptive parents.

Let us examine a few analogies for a moment. When a book is revised, when a newspaper article contains an error that has been corrected, when a tax return is amended, you know changes have been made because a notation appears confirming for the reader information has been adjusted and that this is not an original.

These adoptees' adjusted birth certificates—in my mind—are akin to making counterfeit currency, printing fake checks, offering up a deed on a home that lists you as the owner when you are not or ... I don't know ... it's akin to ... let's say ... falsifying a life. And the egregiousness of it comes from the truth being withheld.

And the original details *do* remain on file; the catch is you have to know there is a different set of details that exists so you can then request your original birth certificate, but that is not possible if you are not told you are adopted. That cannot happen if do not know that there is another truth to your existence.

And because of the comparisons I draw here, knowing that is just how an adoption may be handled—that key details such as my name and who gave birth to me can be changed with the stroke of a pen and those details offered up in a document that looks as official as a university degree—it makes me feel less than ...

Less than human.

It feels like I was regarded and treated as chattel—as property or as an inanimate object that can be shifted from one hand to another, given any label of choice by adults making the decisions with no regard for how this will impact me at any point in the future.

Some may say this was all done for my good; this was designed to protect me from another reality that, quite honestly, may have been worse than I could have imagined. I say otherwise.

It feels like it is all about protecting the adults and giving them what they want. While they are well-meaning efforts, what about the questions the child will have, doubts that swirl in the head, and the confusions that are sure to surface. How does any of this impact the child?

On some levels, though, I get it.

Here is the lay of the land as I see it with absolutely no sugar-coating: The State of Texas had a black girl who had been a ward of the state for more than two years since she had been given up for adoption by her biological mother (the why behind that is another story). There is also a couple that wants a child (or at least one-half of the couple wants a child, but let's ignore the fact that both the father-to-be and the mother-to-be are not collectively 100% all-in). This sounds like a good match. We have two answers to two challenges—a child for a childless couple and parents for a parentless child. Let us put together a birth certificate, send her off with these new parents, tell them to never breathe a word to her about the adoption as a means of protecting her, and keep it moving. That's my *Reader's Digest* interpretation.

But how does that sit with you? Perhaps for some, this is perfectly fine. Some may say, "You had a roof over your head, food on the table, and someone to wipe your behind. What's the problem?"

Understand this. I am not angry. I am not bitter.

I *am* disappointed.

I am hurt. I am frustrated that—for me, through my eyes, from my perspective—the supposed good that was performed overshadows everything else.

Nonetheless, on the surface, I was content, focused and dedicated to my studies, acting as if everything in the world of Bridgett was a-okay when I was at school, and I did my best to be the obedient child who lived a façade of happiness with a commitment to my family.

But I was anything but happy.

My childhood was filled with codeswitching where I used one vernacular that aligned with what was spoken in the house in which I lived, and in school and among friends, I used another vernacular that better aligned with the way I wanted to be perceived and heard by others. Keep I mind, I did not know I was adopted, but I knew there was something different about me, and I would even joke to childhood friends that I believed I was adopted.

To get away from the house, I sought out any extracurricular activities the school system offered that were not too expensive—

... marching, concert, and jazz band although I was a *horrible* trumpet player. (But you would never know it with how I held my head so ridiculously high. Besides, I could not succumb to the alternative where not only did I play horribly but I also looked a mess, so I chose to mask the performance by giving the appearance of utmost confidence. I take some solace, though, in the fact I actually became an incredible baritone player during one high school concert season.)

... U.I.L. prose, poetry, and news and headline writing competitions. (Headline writing was totally my jam! People laugh when I tell them I won first place in that division at a state U.I.L. competition, and I have the letterman jacket patches to prove it!)

.... journalism to include the school newspaper and yearbook committees. (I wonder if that hilarious newspaper column, "Shabba Says," is still around?! It was the brainchild of a rockstar classmate who went on to graduate from Howard University and work in politics.)

... track and field. (Place an emphasis on "field;" I was no runner and competed in shot put.)

Unlike most other children, for me, misery would creep in as the last day of school approached. With summertime on the horizon, this meant I had three months of life ahead that would feel more like three *years* without my much-loved academic and extra-curricular escapes from the house in which I lived.

There are significant decisions I made based on who I *thought* I was—who my birth certificate said I was, who I thought was my family, how I thought my family regarded me and the ways in which they engaged with me, and what I thought were my origins; these are choices that I know would have been different, significantly altering my life path had I been told the truth before having to find out about it on my own in December 2006. (Yes, that's another story, too!)

Am I happy with my life now? Absolutely!

Do I wonder what if …? Most definitely!

Are there days when I question everything—everything about my existence, my purpose, my future, my philosophy about life.

Sure.

How do I keep moving forward?

I just do.

I have two options: I can sit and feel sorry for myself and what could have been, or I can press on and not look back.

I can feel bamboozled or like I was a helpless pawn, or I can work to get beyond the embarrassment and pain to create a reality of which I can be proud.

I can have a "woe is me" attitude, or I can have a "whoa—look at me!" attitude.

With every circumstance, you have options. What you choose is what will dictate if you are resigned to a life of trials or a life of triumphs.

Bridgett's Triumph + Advice

Avoid worrying about what could have been or what should have been. Give as little energy as possible to who wronged you, led you astray, or who you believe did not act in your best interest. None of it may have been intentional. They may have done the best they could with the information, abilities, and resources at their disposal. They may have had fears themselves. They may have also been wronged at some point, led astray, or did not have their own much-needed advocates.

However, if you find yourself in a position where you believe you have been wronged, this script from Terri

Broussard Williams's *Find Your Fire: Stories and Strategies to Inspire the Changemaker Inside You* is the perfect template for speaking up when you believe you have been aggrieved—intentionally or otherwise:

'... I know ... you don't mean (fill in the blank) because you really want the best for me. But I have to tell you what I'm experiencing at this moment is (fill in the blank), and I know you wouldn't do that. Am I right?'

Focus on how you show up in life each day and how you know you deserve to be treated. Endeavor to face the world as the absolute best version of yourself, knowing you brought happiness in the lives of everyone who crossed your path, knowing you created a positive impact, knowing you gave more than you took, knowing you uplifted others more than you tore them down, knowing you spread more smiles than frowns.

But what if you have not always followed that pattern? What if you are not known for that type of existence? Is it fraudulent to now show up as such?

Not at all. It is a new day, and you can be a new person. You can shift gears. You can press the reset button. You can change directions. You make your own rules. You can rise above the trials.

In order to do so, though, do not allow yourself to get mired in what does not go right or what does not go your way because there will be some days when, for one or two minutes, the sunshine, puppies, and rainbows go into hiding. This is not to suggest you should expect the trials to come and that you should simply accept and embrace them with no regard for how they make you feel. This *is* to affirm that you should not allow any circumstance to define you or—worse yet—let it detain you.

You should not let it get you stuck to the point you are not advancing or to the point where you are not making strides to live up to your potential.

For a long time, I thought I was "a certain person" with a certain background and a certain lineage, and as such, I put limits on myself because of from whence I thought I came. Hold the phone. Let me be very clear: my biological family is not sitting in a castle on thrones, wearing tiaras and crowns. However, I cannot help but to wonder "what if" because, quite honestly, I feel like I have no identify. Sure, as a professional speaker, many have seen me on stages as a confident being with a strong voice coupled with seemingly boundless conviction and unshakable confidence, and that's all real talk. It is the real me. However, I have moments when I am reminded that I do not have a relative in my circle I can look at and see myself in her or him. I wonder if I may have passed a relative on a street or in an air- port as I traverse from one city to another on business or vacation. (And I *did* run into a biological relative at a conference in 2018 in San Diego! I seldom wear my conference name badge, but that day, I was fortunate that other conference-goers do! But that is another story!)

My point is in the midst of all my rhetoric in conviction and confidence, there is no one to whom I can turn to understand why I am the way I am, why I talk the way I talk, laugh the way I laugh, think the way I think ...

I am a McGowen on paper (and on the speaker stage but a McGowen-Hawkins by marriage), and I grew up acting in ways I thought was acceptable for a McGowen; however, I never felt I could be myself, which in reality, I do not really know what the heck that is. (I recall a sixth-grade science teacher even commenting at one meet-the-teacher night "I've had other McGowens come through my class, and she's nothing like them!" I was struck by that statement in a number of ways. One, I deemed it a compliment because I top performer in the class, and the teacher was consistently pleased with my work. And, two, I had seen and felt the difference myself and wondered what was it that made me different from all the other McGowens he had seen. I wondered if others, like that science teacher, saw it, too. And if they did see it, what did that mean? Were they all keeping it a secret? If so, then why? Why was I the only one in the dark?

Again, I am a McGowen on paper; however, what does that mean? McGowen is not just my adoptive family's last name; it is the last name of my adoptive family's ancestors' slave owner. It was the last name given them after their original identity—like countless other blacks in this country who have histories that are tied to and steeped in slavery—had been stripped from them. Therefore, whenever I write my name, not only is it not the name that appeared on my first and original birth certificate, and not only is it not my biological family's name; but It is the last name of a slave owner. Read: As a black person in America, I have an even deeper loss of identity.

Nonetheless, I made the safe choice of doing, thinking, and being what I thought my adoptive parents wanted to see in me. But what if I had known differently—more specifically—what if I had known the truth?

How would personal, academic, and professional decisions have been impacted? What identity would I have created for myself as opposed to being who I thought my adoptive parents wanted me to be? What would I have attempted that I stopped myself from even *thinking* of trying to do simply because of who I *thought* I was?

Is my life terrible?

Absolutely not.

Not by any stretch of the imagination has my life amounted to anything of which I am not proud.

But is there a gnawing feeling in the back of my mind that resurfaces from time to time and has me pondering who I am, why me, and what if? Certainly.

Are there days when it stops me in my tracks? You bet.

Do I find myself looking at nothing in particular, reflecting on the years that led up to finally knowing the truth, the years that followed and struggling to make sense of the truth and who in the world I am, and the years it took to finally get as many pieces of the story surrounding my adoption as I could to position me to arrive at a point where I can say "I'm adopted" without feeling uncomfortable or strangely inadequate?

Without question.

Hold your head as high as you can. Speak with strength and fortitude. Focus on projecting to the world the person you would want to see smiling back at you if you passed you on the street. Let everyone know there is no stopping you, that you may not be perfect, and that's perfectly okay. Shine your light. Do not dim it. And do not back down. Break through the limitations—real and perceived. Leave the past where it is, and set your sights on all the triumphs that are to come because trust me. They are on their way.

Bianca Chandler, author of *70 Days, 70 Ways: He Speaks to Me*, puts it best when she writes "Never allow your environment to define you. Trust God's ability to transform what the world expects you to become and replace it with what He has destined for you to be. Remember, tragedy can translate to triumph—even when you are uncomfortable, He is working. When you feel beaten up and battered, He is still working. Even in your emptiest and most gruesome moments, God still sees a vessel."

Know there is a power greater than you who has a plan with which no one on earth can interfere. Live not for this world but for what you were destined to be. Do you. Be you. Be triumphant.

Bridgett's Bio

"Talks too much" was a comment Bridgett McGowen consistently received on her elementary school report cards. Early on, she developed a love for speaking, words, and books—so much so until she was always the first to volunteer to read passages aloud in class, and during moments of boredom in her third- and fourth-grade classes, she would analyze the dictionary, jotting down those words and definitions she found particularly interesting.

With reading as a favorite pastime and little to no fear for speaking in front of a crowd, it only makes sense that Bridgett is now an award-winning international professsional speaker and the CEO of BMcTALKS Press, an independent publishing company where she thrives in an environment where she gets to bring other people's words to life. Bridgett's résumé also includes being a 2019-2020 member of Forbes Coaches Council launching BMcTALKS Academy where, as the founder and owner, she helps professionals use their voices to monetize their expertise.

Since 2001, Bridgett has been a professional speaker and has spoken on programs alongside prominent figures such as former President Barack Obama, Deepak Chopra,

Alex Rodriguez (A-Rod), Oprah Winfrey, Shonda Rhimes, Katie Couric, Chip Gaines, and Janelle Monáe.

The prestigious University of Texas at Austin presented her with a Master Presenter Award in 2006; Canada-based One Woman has presented her with two Fearless Woman Awards; and she has facilitated hundreds of workshops, keynote and commencement addresses, conference sessions, trainings, and webinars to thousands of students and professionals who are positioned all around the globe.

Bridgett's expertise and presentations have been sought after by companies, post-secondary institutions, and organizations such as Society for Human Resource Management (SHRM), Vanguard Investments, Norton LifeLock, Symantec, Kentucky Fried Chicken, McGraw-Hill Education, LinkedIn Local, Association for Talent Development (ATD), Doña Ana Community College, National Association of Women Sales Professionals, Independence University, Turnitin, Texas Healthcare Trustees, Prairie View A&M University, Orbis Education, and National Association of Black Accountants.

Forbes, LinkedIn, and Thrive Global are a few of the platforms where you can find articles penned by Bridgett. In addition, she has been quoted by Transizion, has contributed to UpJourney, and has appeared as a guest on The Training and Learning Development Company's TLDCast, Phoenix Business Radio, and a multitude of podcasts to showcase her expertise in the professional speaking industry. Her work has been highlighted by *VoyagePhoenix Magazine*; award-winning branding and consulting agency, Catalyst; The Startup Growth; and her alma mater, Prairie View A&M University (PVAMU), the second oldest institution of higher education in the state of Texas and a part of the Texas A&M University System.

Bridgett has also taught for PVAMU, Lone Star College System, and University of Phoenix. She graduated cum laude with her bachelor's degree in communication, and one year later, she graduated summa cum laude with her master's degree. She is a Forbes contributor; a member of International Society of Female Professionals; a member of Alpha Kappa Alpha Sorority, Incorporated; a publisher; and was the 2018-2020 president of her local Toastmasters International club.

In 2019, Bridgett authored and published two books, *REAL TALK: What Other Experts Won't Tell You About How to Make Presentations That Sizzle* as well as *Rise and Sizzle: Daily Communication and Presentation Strategies for Sales, Business, and Higher Ed Pros*, the former of which sold out within minutes of her presentation concluding at ATD's 76th annual international conference and exposition in Washington, D.C.

In January 2020, she also wrote and published *Show Up and Show Out: 52 Communication Habits to Make You Unforgettable*, which sold out at the annual Think Better Live Better event hosted in February 2020 in San Diego, California by *New York Times* best-sellers Marc and Angel Chernoff. Days later, she published *Own the Microphone: How 50 of the World's Best Professional Speakers Launched Their Careers (and How You Can, Too!)* Her next compilation, *Redesign Your 9-to-5*, as well as her first podcast are both due for summer 2020 releases.

Bridgett's mission is to help professionals turn their voices into powerhouses to inspire millions and build serious skill sets that will lead to more and more opportunities.

Bridgett is married to the most amazing Aaron Hawkins, and she gives so much credit to him for being her greatest cheerleader and for reminding her every day how important and special she is to him, their family, and the world. Bridgett resides in the Phoenix, Arizona area with her family, enjoys frequent summertime get-aways to San Diego, and she absolutely loves beautiful sunsets.

Post a Review

Please leave your feedback on reading this book.

1. Visit www.amazon.com
2. Type in the search field the book title, "Triumph Over the Trials," along with the last name, "McGowen"
3. Scroll down, and click on "Write a customer review"

Let me know what you thought of the book and what you gained from it.

I read every review. They are tremendously helpful! Thank you!

www.ingramcontent.com/pod-product-compliance
Lightning Source LLC
Chambersburg PA
CBHW030452010526
44118CB00011B/899